THE JESUS
PAUL KNEW

10 STUDIES FOR INDIVIDUALS OR GROUPS

LifeGuide®
BIBLE STUDIES

JAMES W. REAPSOME

IVP Connect
An imprint of InterVarsity Press
Downers Grove, Illinois

InterVarsity Press
P.O. Box 1400, Downers Grove, IL 60515-1426
ivpress.com
email@ivpress.com

InterVarsity Press® is the book-publishing division of InterVarsity Christian Fellowship/USA®, a
movement of students and faculty active on campus at hundreds of universities, colleges and schools
of nursing in the United States of America, and a member movement of the International Fellowship
of Evangelical Students. For information about local and regional activities, visit intervarsity.org.

LifeGuide® is a registered trademark of InterVarsity Christian Fellowship.

All Scripture quotations, unless otherwise indicated, are taken from THE HOLY BIBLE, NEW
INTERNATIONAL VERSION®, NIV® Copyright © 1973, 1978, 1984, 2011 by Biblica, Inc.™ Used by
permission. All rights reserved worldwide.

While all stories in this book are true, some names and identifying information in this book may have
been changed to protect the privacy of the individuals involved.

Cover design: Cindy Kiple
Cover image: © Evelina Kremsdorf / Trevillion Images

ISBN 978-0-8308-3113-5 (print)
ISBN 978-0-8308-6324-2 (digital)

Printed in the United States of America ♾

InterVarsity Press is committed to ecological stewardship and to the conservation of natural
resources in all our operations. This book was printed using sustainably sourced paper.

P 25 24 23 22 21 20 19 18 17 16 15 14 13 12 11 10 9 8 7 6 5 4 3 2 1

Y 40 39 38 37 36 35 34 33 32 31 30 29 28 27 26 25 24 23 22 21 20 19 18

Contents

Getting the Most Out of
The Jesus Paul Knew

The apostle Paul experienced an extraordinary encounter with Jesus that changed the trajectory of his life. In Scripture, we witness Paul learning more about Jesus—about his remarkable grace, peace, power, love, and sacrifice—and then passionately sharing his message with others. This passion is what eventually led Paul to declare, "For me, to live is Christ. To die is gain" (Philippians 1:21).

In recent years, scholars have tended to focus more on Paul's foundational theology, but we can learn so much from Paul and what it looks like to obey Jesus in the everyday tests of faith.

Suggestions for Individual Study

1. As you begin each study, pray that God will speak to you through his Word.

2. Read the introduction to the study and respond to the personal reflection question or exercise. This is designed to help you focus on God and on the theme of the study.

3. Each study deals with a particular passage so that you can delve into the author's meaning in that context. Read and reread the passage to be studied. The questions are written using the language of the New International Version, so you may wish to use that version of the Bible. The New Revised Standard Version is also recommended.

4. This is an inductive Bible study, designed to help you discover for yourself what Scripture is saying. The study includes three types of questions. *Observation* questions ask about the basic facts: who, what, when, where, and how. *Interpretation* questions delve into the meaning of the passage. *Application* questions help you discover the implications of the text for growing in Christ. These three keys unlock the treasures of Scripture.

Write your answers to the questions in the spaces provided or in a personal journal. Writing can bring clarity and deeper understanding of yourself and of God's Word.

5. It might be good to have a Bible dictionary handy. Use it to look up any unfamiliar words, names, or places.

6. Use the prayer suggestion to guide you in thanking God for what you have learned and to pray about the applications that have come to mind.

7. You may want to go on to the suggestion under "Now or Later," or you may want to use that idea for your next study.

Suggestions for Members of a Group Study

1. Come to the study prepared. Follow the suggestions for individual study mentioned above. You will find that careful preparation will greatly enrich your time spent in group discussion.

2. Be willing to participate in the discussion. The leader of your group will not be lecturing. Instead, he or she will be encouraging the members of the group to discuss what they have learned. The leader will be asking the questions that are found in this guide.

3. Stick to the topic being discussed. Your answers should be based on the verses that are the focus of the discussion and not on outside authorities such as commentaries or speakers. These studies focus on a particular passage of Scripture. Only rarely should you refer to other portions of the Bible. This allows for everyone to participate in in-depth study on equal ground.

4. Be sensitive to the other members of the group. Listen attentively when they describe what they have learned. You may be surprised by their insights! Each question assumes a variety of answers. Many questions do not have "right" answers, particularly questions that aim at meaning or application. Instead the questions push us to explore the passage more thoroughly.

When possible, link what you say to the comments of others. Also, be affirming whenever you can. This will encourage some of the more hesitant members of the group to participate.

5. Be careful not to dominate the discussion. We are sometimes so eager to express our thoughts that we leave too little opportunity for others to respond. By all means participate! But allow others to also.

6. Expect God to teach you through the passage being discussed and through the other members of the group. Pray that you will have an enjoyable and profitable time together, but also that as a result of the study you will find ways that you can take action individually and/or as a group.

7. Remember that anything said in the group is considered confidential and should not be discussed outside the group unless specific permission is given to do so.

8. If you are the group leader, you will find additional suggestions at the back of the guide.

1

Source of Grace

For many people, the quality of grace brings out feelings of love and forgiveness. My niece's son received what we thought was an unusually severe sentence for his felony. We kept hoping and praying that his sentence would be reduced, which eventually it was. He had become a Christian while in prison, and grace took on an entirely new meaning for him. He was beginning to understand something about God and his grace. *Grace* is more than a theological idea because it moves people to change and give God glory. The apostle Paul found grace in Jesus, which changed him forever.

GROUP DISCUSSION. Christians have been called the recipients of "cheap grace." In what way might this accusation be fair? How do you respond to this charge?

PERSONAL REFLECTION. When you receive the gift of God's grace as Paul did, how does it make you feel? What changes should God's grace bring about in you?

The setting of Paul's letters to Timothy are intensely personal. Paul wants to teach his young protégé what it means to be a pastor and evangelist. We ought to study and discover the Jesus

Paul knew so we might be better prepared to worship and serve Jesus in our everyday lives, not just to become a professional church leader. *Read 1 Timothy 1:1-2, 12-17.*

1. What points about Jesus does Paul want to make clear in his greeting to Timothy (vv. 1-2)?

2. Why were these points critical to understanding his relationship with Jesus?

3. Can you identify with any of these facts about Jesus? Explain.

4. For what three things was Paul grateful to Jesus for providing a foundation for their life together (v. 12)?

5. What gifts from Jesus had overcome Paul's past (vv. 13-14)?

6. In what ways have these gifts changed your life and built your confidence in Jesus?

_____

7. Why did Jesus come to our world (v. 15)?

_____

8. Why did Jesus show his mercy to Paul (v. 16)?

_____

9. How can you help to display Christ's patience to others (v. 16)?

_____

10. How does Paul's benediction help us to better understand the Jesus Paul knew (v. 17)?

Ask God to help you overcome your past and make a fresh start with Jesus.

Now or Later

Find a good book about Paul's life with Jesus and keep a notebook of your new ideas. You might try John Pollock, *The Apostle: A Life of Paul*, 3rd ed. (Colorado Springs, CO: Cook, 2012), or Jim Reapsome, *The Imitation of Saint Paul: Examining Our Lives in Light of His Example* (Eugene, OR: Cascade, 2013).

2

Visionary Leader

Acts 26

Visionary leaders have left their mark on history. Some of them were spiritually minded, like Joan of Arc, but many others were simply politically motivated and gave God the credit for their empires. The Holy Roman Empire exerted both religious and political power. Ordinary Christians among the peasants easily accepted their leaders' claims to divine power and authority.

Closer to our time, people have been led by Mother Teresa, Mohandas Gandhi, and Martin Luther King Jr., as well as by wicked visionaries like Adolf Hitler, Joseph Stalin, and Mao Zedong. Paul's vision of his commission by Jesus extended to what we might call his spiritual empire or leadership among the new churches he founded.

GROUP DISCUSSION. How has your knowledge of church and political history affected your approach to Jesus and the gospel?

PERSONAL REFLECTION. How does learning to know Jesus, as Paul did, affect your thinking and action in secular affairs.

Our study takes us to a dramatic scene worthy of a movie plot. A relatively unknown evangelist in the process of turning the world upside down testified before a Roman puppet king. Paul makes his purpose clear and ties everything to Jesus. *Read Acts 26.*

1. Describe the setting in which Paul confessed to receiving his assignment from Jesus (vv. 1-8).

2. Why was it crucial for Paul to make his relationship with Jesus clear in this context?

3. When have you been more or less forced to confess your relationship with Jesus?

4. What basic assignment did Paul receive from Jesus (vv. 12-18)?

What was its scope?

Its content?

5. Why would this assignment have been so revolutionary for him to accept?

6. How would you have reacted to Jesus if you had been in Paul's shoes? Why?

7. What contemporary obstacles stand in your way of doing what Jesus tells you to do?

8. In what ways does the life and mission of your church look similar to Paul's commission from Jesus?

9. What happened when Paul publicly carried out his basic assignment (vv. 19-23)?

10. How can you and your church stick wholeheartedly to Paul's message?

Pray for one another to have courage to obey Jesus.

Now or Later

Make plans with a fellow Christian to help one another with evangelistic outreach.

3

Comfort in Dark Times

Philippians 1:12-26

My own dark times began with the loss of my wife. When our daughter was two, my wife suffered an aneurysm and died shortly after giving birth to our son, who died in childbirth. But, like Paul, I also found comfort in Jesus. He made the difference. He had promised his disciples peace and even joy when the hard times hit them (John 16:31-33). Discovering Jesus as Paul did became a watershed event in my life.

GROUP DISCUSSION. Have you walked through dark times with Jesus? How have you helped someone walk through their dark times with Jesus?

PERSONAL REFLECTION. Jesus wanted to make Paul like himself (Romans 8:29). What steps are you taking in that direction?

The setting of Philippians is Paul's imprisonment in Rome. He had helped to start a church in Philippi. These new Christians became his strong friends and stood by him. They were his means of comfort in dark times. *Read Philippians 1:12-26.*

1. What positive spin did Paul put on his imprisonment (vv. 12-14)?

2. How did Paul's relationship with Jesus keep him from caving in to fear and depression?

3. To be a voice for Jesus, what did Paul have to gain from their relationship?

4. In what situations have you felt that you were symbolically "in chains for Christ" (v. 13)?

5. What caused Paul to rejoice (vv. 15-18)?

6. How does the cause of his joy relate to his basic assignment from Jesus (see also study 2)?

7. What was one of Paul's objectives in his relationship with Jesus (vv. 19-21)?

8. What had he learned about Jesus (vv. 22-23)?

9. How can your boasting in Christ "abound" in the Christian community (vv. 24-26)?

10. How can you bring "progress and joy in the faith" (v. 25) to fellow Christians by your relationship with Jesus?

Pray for someone in your circle who is going through dark times.

Now or Later

Read a good book on comforting people in grief, or use the LifeGuide Bible study on grief.

4

The Peacemaker

Peacemakers are highly valued on the political circuit. And Nobel prizes go to peacemakers: Martin Luther King Jr., Mother Teresa, Lech Wałęsa, and Nelson Mandela, for example. Each major religion claims its peacemakers. I watched the Dalai Lama speak to the World's Parliament of Religions, and as he was leaving the auditorium he was immersed in a crowd of mothers and babies begging for his peace and blessing. Only the story of Jesus, however, claims to bring peace with God on the basis of a personal Savior's death. He is the world's supreme reconciler. The apostle Paul urges us to be reconciled with God. The war is over; lay down your arms because peace has been declared only through Christ.

GROUP DISCUSSION. What keeps nations at war? What keeps individuals from finding peace and joy?

PERSONAL REFLECTION. When have you been at war with God? What does it mean for you to be reconciled with God?

In his second letter to the church at Corinth, Paul reveals more of what he learned about Jesus. He is intensely personal, even when teaching them some basic theology based on Christ's peacemaking mission to the world. *Read 2 Corinthians 5:11-21.*

---

1. Read the entire passage and list all the facts Paul learned about Jesus.

---

2. How do you think Jesus communicated his love to Paul?

---

3. What did it mean for Paul to be "in Christ," and what was the result of their new relationship (v. 17)?

---

4. Share some ways it can be said that you are "in Christ."

---

5. Why is our reconciliation with God necessary (vv. 19, 21)?

6. What contemporary synonyms for *reconciliation* can shed light on its meaning?

---

7. Why do you think Jesus called Paul an "ambassador"?

---

8. In what sense are Christians ambassadors for Jesus?

---

9. What picture do you get of Paul's knowing Jesus from his plea, "We implore you on Christ's behalf" (v. 20)?

---

10. How does Paul's command "Be reconciled to God" (v. 20) help you to understand Jesus' direction for your life?

Pray for those finding it hard to be Christ's ambassador.

Now or Later

Look for ways your group can serve Jesus in peace making.

5

Demanding Everything

Philippians 3:1-14

Probably nothing in life is more demanding than joining the military. When I stepped across the line at my induction center, I swore not only to defend my country but to uphold the US Constitution and obey my commander in chief. Suddenly I realized my life didn't belong to me. It was controlled by people I had never met and later by corporals and sergeants I came to know well and who demanded everything I thought was my own.

By demanding everything, the Army was training me for unquestioned obedience. Our lives depended on this. Paul's relationship with Jesus was like that. He knew that Jesus wanted everything. Even our family loyalties have to give way to the demands of Jesus (Luke 14:25-27).

Along the way I met Jesus my Lord, and I looked to him for ultimate direction in my life. A personal crisis had crushed me, and I learned that Jesus demanded everything—even my golf clubs and fishing rods had to go.

GROUP DISCUSSION. Discuss everything and everyone who puts demands on your life. Which demands are you happy to accept, and which do you reject? Why?

PERSONAL REFLECTION. The Christian classic *Have We No Rights?* by Mabel Williamson has changed many people. What rights do you want to hold on to? Why?

Paul gave up all his rights when he met Jesus. His commitment cost him many painful encounters, including time in prison in Rome and being separated from his beloved friends in Philippi, who played a major role in his learning to know Jesus. *Read Philippians 3:1-14.*

1. What issue was troubling the Christians in Philippi (vv. 1-4)?

2. How did Paul define his former confidence in the flesh (vv. 4-6)?

3. Describe any parallels to this issue in your life and your church.

4. Pretend you are interviewing Paul. Ask him to tell you exactly what he had lost and what he had found. What do you think he would say?

5. What value did Paul place on knowing Jesus (vv. 7-8)?

6. How would you describe the value of your knowledge of Jesus?

_____

7. What did Paul gain from knowing Jesus?

_____

8. Contrast two kinds of "righteousness" (v. 9). Which one did Paul follow, and what did he learn about Jesus and keeping the law?

_____

9. How does your knowledge of Jesus shape your spiritual aspirations (vv. 10-11)?

_____

10. What does knowing the power of Christ's resurrection and sharing in his sufferings look like in your life?

Pray for those who want to be like Paul and know the power of Christ's resurrection.

Now or Later

Seek the friendship of some older, wiser Christians who can guide you in the direction Jesus was taking with Paul.

6

Lover and Protector

"Lover and protector" would fit the themes of many novels, movies, and televisions shows well. It also accurately depicts the life of the Jesus Paul came to know. But the stuff of fiction cannot match the scope of Christ's love and protection. Nothing comes close to the power and love of Jesus, who said, "I give them eternal life, and they shall never perish; no one will snatch them out of my hand" (John 10:28). This is the Jesus Paul came to know at the deepest levels of his being. One of my student Bible study groups wrestled with Christ's promise of love and protection. What if they broke one of God's commands or failed to acknowledge Christ publicly? Paul thought about things much worse and yet emerged as a spiritual conqueror.

GROUP DISCUSSION. How does the image of lover and protector fit your understanding of Jesus? What other images of Jesus do you have? How can Christians best help others come to a deeper relationship with Christ as Paul did?

PERSONAL REFLECTION. Chart the time you spend with Jesus. Where does time with him fit in your priorities?

Romans 8 is where Paul changes direction in his letter to the Romans. Now his theology demands application to life. How better to begin than to show how Jesus leads us safely through the storms of life. *Read Romans 8:31-39.*

1. What had Paul come to understand when he came to know Jesus (v. 32)?

2. What meaning did the death, resurrection, and exaltation of Jesus have for Paul (vv. 33-34)?

3. Why do you think Paul raised the problem of being separated from Jesus (v. 35)?

Why did he ask *who* rather than *what* might separate him from Christ's love?

4. When has the feeling of losing Christ's love been a problem for you? Why?

5. What experiences could possibly cut off Paul's relationship with Jesus (v. 35)?

Why wasn't Paul overwhelmed by them (v. 36)?

6. How did the love of Jesus transform Paul (v. 37)?

---

7. How does your walk in the love of Jesus make you more than a conqueror (v. 37)?

---

8. Express in your own words everything the love of Jesus protects you from (vv. 38-39)?

---

9. How does Paul's knowledge of Jesus as his lover and protector expand from verse 35 to verses 38-39?

How would this lift his spirit and determination?

---

10. How do your suffering and hardship strengthen your knowledge of Jesus?

Pray for others who live in fear of things to come.

Now or Later

Read stories from church and missions history about Christians who were "more than conquerors." What did you learn?

7

Choosing the Cross

1 Corinthians 1:18-31; 2:1-5

After he met Jesus and surrendered to him, Paul realized that the best the Jews and the Greeks had to offer was utter nonsense compared to God's revelation in Christ. In one seemingly preposterous act—the death of Christ on the cross—God had obliterated "the wisdom of the world."

Some people considered to be wise still scoff at the cross and ridicule the proposition that God has redeemed humanity by Christ's sacrifice. But while some people laugh at the cross, God has the last laugh. Paul saw through the imposing structure of religious philosophy and speculation. He rightly discerned that the best of human wisdom could never accomplish salvation and eternal life.

Paul met Jesus and propounded a simple, clear idea that blew away anything the Greeks had to offer: the man, Jesus of Nazareth in Galilee (a Roman province), had been nailed to a cross in Jerusalem and rose from the dead, so that anyone—Jew or Greek— might have eternal salvation in him. Christ's crucifixion loomed as the crucial, distinctive component of Paul's life and ministry.

GROUP DISCUSSION. Why does the world at large still turn away from the crucified Savior? Among what population sectors have you found a faith response? Why?

PERSONAL REFLECTION. In what settings do you find it best to worship Jesus and believe in his death and resurrection? Why?

Paul's personal reflection in this letter to the church at Corinth makes it clear that the cross was a choice, no matter how much this idea clashed with current pagan and Jewish ideas. His letter showed he stood for the cross of Jesus in the swirl of a fierce cultural and religious battle. *Read 1 Corinthians 1:18-31; 2:1-5.*

1. In what religious and social context did Paul learn to know Jesus (vv. 18-25)?

2. What major truths about Jesus did Paul follow and preach?

3. What was the point of Paul's linking himself with someone whose ministry was foolishness and a stumbling block?

4. What contemporary ideas force you to evaluate your view of Christ crucified?

How do you settle the issue?

5. Contrast "Christ crucified" and "Christ the power of God and wisdom of God" (vv. 23-24). How do you think Paul reconciled these sharp differences in his walk with Jesus?

_____

6. Why was it important and valuable for Paul to learn that in Christ, God chose his followers from among the foolish, weak, and lowly (vv. 26-29)?

Would you be inclined to trust and obey someone whose crowd looked like the foolish, weak, and lowly Corinthians? Why?

_____

7. How did being in Christ benefit Paul (v. 30)?

_____

8. In what sense was Paul boasting in Jesus (v. 31)?

Does your Christian life boast in the Lord? Explain.

9. List all the influences on Paul's ministry as a result of his knowing Jesus crucified (1 Corinthians 2:1-5).

How did this shape both his delivery and his content?

---

10. What steps can you take to follow Jesus and Paul according to verse 2?

Pray for Christians who lack self-confidence. Ask God to build them up in Christ.

Now or Later

Visit an art museum and spend time meditating on classic paintings of Jesus on the cross.

8

Giver of Strength and Contentment

Philippians 4:10-20

Imagine sitting in Starbucks in Philippi with your friends and reading together this letter from Paul, who was imprisoned. Questions pop up from all quarters: "Is Paul, okay? How's he getting along? Did he get our gift? What about his trial?" Did any of them inquire about Paul's spiritual strength? Did anyone ask if his faith had buckled under pressure?

Earlier in his letter, Paul had assured the Christians in Philippi that the gospel was advancing in Rome in spite of adverse circumstances (Philippians 1:12). Before signing off, he addressed their fears for his overall personal welfare. The Philippians probably choked when they read his closing words. Tears welled up in their eyes when he said he was more than all right; he was actually contented.

Had I been there, I would have felt a knife plunging into my heart. Paul contented? How could that possibly be true? If he is contented in prison, why am I griping and complaining about my aches and pains, my children, my boss, some of my fellow believers? I would have swallowed hard under the Holy Spirit's conviction.

As quickly as Paul's readers scratched their heads and asked, "How can this be true?" Paul revealed his secret in two stages. First, the power of the risen Christ living in him: "I can do all this through him who gives me strength" (Philippians 4:13). This was the key that opened the door to his deep knowledge of Jesus. Second, the practical assistance sent to him by his sisters and brothers at Philippi.

GROUP DISCUSSION. How does our culture profit from our discontentment? What issues of weakness call for strength beyond what society has to offer?

PERSONAL REFLECTION. What keeps you from contentment? What about your family and friends?

The setting here is probably the most deeply personal of Paul's letters. The power and love Paul found in Jesus were something very enlightening both to Paul and the Philippians. *Read Philippians 4:10-20.*

1. What had the Philippians done to cause Paul to write them about his contentment (vv. 14-18)?

2. Share with your group opportunities you have had to do the same.

3. How did Paul summarize "whatever the circumstances" (vv. 11-12)?

4. Define the scope and details of Paul's life for which he needed strength (v. 13).

5. In what areas of your life do you feel a particular need for strength?

6. Who gave Paul his strength (Philippians 3:12-14)? Strength for what?

7. What is the connection between having contentment and having strength?

8. Paul was thankful for Christ's strength. What other things helped him to find contentment (vv. 14, 18)?

9. What "riches . . . in Christ" met Paul's needs (v. 19)?

What might have been some of the needs among the Philippians?

---

10. Do you feel you have discovered the secret to contentment from this passage? Why or why not?

How can you give glory to God for the strength and peace of Christ you now enjoy (v. 20)?

Pray for those finding it difficult to be fully content in Jesus.

Now or Later

Make a list of contented Christians you know. Write what you believe are their secrets of success.

9

Jesus or Nothing

Galatians 1:1-9; 2:20-21

"Greater love has no one than this: to lay down one's life for one's friends," Jesus told his disciples (John 15:13). US Navy Chaplain George Rentz did that while the USS Houston was sinking after taking a hit from Japanese forces during the Battle of Sunda Strait in March 1942.

During the abandonment of the sinking Houston, Chaplain Rentz entered the water and attained partial safety. He attempted to relinquish his space and lifejacket to wounded survivors nearby. He declared, "You men are young, I have lived the major part of my life and I am willing to go."* He ultimately relinquished his lifejacket to Seaman First Class Walter L. Beeson. When Beeson realized that Rentz was gone, he put on the lifejacket.** For these actions, Rentz was posthumously awarded the United States Navy's second highest award for valor, the Navy Cross.

For the chaplain it clearly was a case of Jesus or nothing. He found the same truth about Jesus that Paul did, and it cost him his life. Being ready and willing to go is the fruit of a deep love for and obedience to Christ.

GROUP DISCUSSION. How do you explain such examples of bravery and heroism? Why is Jesus always the issue?

PERSONAL REFLECTION. What is one issue you would be willing to give your life for?

Galatians provides further insight to Paul's discovery of Jesus. All that Jesus stood for was at stake. There was no middle ground. *Read Galatians 1:1-9; 2:20-21.*

1. In Paul's greeting, find and discuss what he had learned about Jesus (vv. 1-5).

2. What facts were crucial to Paul and Jesus' relationship?

3. What difference do they make in your life?

4. What difference did it make that his mission with Jesus was not humanly inspired (v. 1)?

5. What had Paul received from Jesus in return for his commitment to him?

6. Without religious jargon, spell out what Jesus has done for you.

7. What false teaching had infected the churches in Galatia (Galatians 2:21)?

8. If this different gospel were true, how would that affect the Jesus-Paul relationship and mission?

9. How does Paul's "crucified . . . but Christ lives in me" (vv. 20-21) experience undercut the phony gospel of trying to please God by works?

10. What does it mean for you to live by faith in the sacrificial love of Jesus?

Pray for those who may be confused about living by faith.

Now or Later

Make a list of "other gospels" that attract people today. Why do false teachers draw wide crowds?

---

*George Rentz, quoted in Duane P. Schultz, *The Last Battle Station* (New York: St. Martin's Press, 1985), 204.

**James G. Hornfischer, *Ship of Ghosts* (New York: Bantam Books, 2006), 156-57.

10

Inspirer of Praise

Ephesians 1:3-14

Since the 1970s Christians have developed some new forms
of praise. The first editions of so-called praise songs hit the
streets, followed by a lot more instrumental accompaniment.
Some critics charged the church with copying contemporary
music styles. It wasn't too long before some Christians fought
over music and congregations split on the issue. It was easy for
them to forget that Jesus said even the rocks would praise him
(Luke 19:40). Such issues did not confront Paul and Jesus. Paul
followed Jesus in battling for truth, not for worship styles. That
is why Paul told the Colossians they should teach one another
with "all wisdom through psalms, hymns, and songs from the
Spirit, singing to God with gratitude in your hearts" (Colossians 3:16). That was the lasting imprint Jesus made on Paul's
life of praise and worship.

GROUP DISCUSSION. Why has music in worship become such a divi-
sive issue? What peaceful solutions have helped to unify worship?

PERSONAL REFLECTION. How does music affect your worship?
Why?

Paul's opening of Ephesians reveals probably his deepest walk with Jesus and how he made sure their relationship grew to the praise of God's glory. Everything in this section shows why Paul was drawn to Jesus. *Read Ephesians 1:3-14.*

---

1. The New International Version of the Bible with paragraph titles calls Paul's story with Jesus here "Praise for Spiritual Blessings in Christ." You can appreciate the impact on Paul's life (and your own as well) by substituting "me" for "us." Pick out all the reasons why your praise is called for.

---

2. In a printed version of the text, underline everything Paul had learned about Jesus.

---

3. How would you define the scope of Paul's blessings?

---

4. Which of the blessings are the most difficult to grasp? Why?

What can you do to make them more easily understood?

5. Paul's walk with Jesus demanded praise and worship (vv. 3, 6, 12, 14). What would your prayer of praise to God look like?

How can you expand your praise horizons?

_____

6. Clearly, Paul wanted to live for what he called the praise of Christ's glory (v. 12). What do you think he means by this?

_____

7. How does this purpose for Paul illuminate the depths of intimacy between him and Jesus?

_____

8. What role did Paul give to the Holy Spirit (vv. 13-14)?

_____

9. How are you liberated by knowing you are "God's possession" (v. 14)?

10. Paul's knowledge of Jesus plumbed the depths of Christian theology. What does this tell you about how you can grow in the grace, love, strength, and knowledge of Jesus?

Pray that divisions over church music would be healed.

Now or Later

Make a list of steps you could to take to come to worship with the right attitude.

Leader's Notes

MY GRACE IS SUFFICIENT FOR YOU. (2 CORINTHIANS 12:9)

Leading a Bible discussion can be an enjoyable and rewarding experience. But it can also be *scary*—especially if you've never done it before. If this is your feeling, you're in good company. When God asked Moses to lead the Israelites out of Egypt, he replied, "Please send someone else" (Exodus 4:13)! It was the same with Solomon, Jeremiah, and Timothy, but God helped these people in spite of their weaknesses, and he will help you as well.

You don't need to be an expert on the Bible or a trained teacher to lead a Bible discussion. The idea behind these inductive studies is that the leader guides group members to discover for themselves what the Bible has to say. This method of learning will allow group members to remember much more of what is said than a lecture would.

These studies are designed to be led easily. As a matter of fact, the flow of questions through the passage from observation to interpretation to application is so natural that you may feel that the studies lead themselves. This study guide is also flexible. You can use it with a variety of groups—student, professional, neighborhood, or church groups. Each study takes forty-five to sixty minutes in a group setting.

There are some important facts to know about group dynamics and encouraging discussion. The suggestions listed below should enable you to effectively and enjoyably fulfill your role as leader.

Preparing for the Study

1. Ask God to help you understand and apply the passage in your own life. Unless this happens, you will not be prepared to lead others. Pray too for the various members of the group. Ask God to open your hearts to the message of his Word and motivate you to action.

2. Read the introduction to the guide to get an overview of the entire book and the issues that will be explored.

3. As you begin each study, read and reread the assigned Bible passage to familiarize yourself with it.

4. This study guide is based on the New International Version of the Bible. It will help you and the group if you use this translation as the basis for your study and discussion.

5. Carefully work through each question in the study. Spend time in meditation and reflection as you consider how to respond.

6. Write your thoughts and responses in the space provided in the study guide. This will help you to express your understanding of the passage clearly.

7. It might help to have a Bible dictionary handy. Use it to look up any unfamiliar words, names, or places. (For additional help on how to study a passage, see chapter five of *How to Lead a LifeGuide Bible Study,* InterVarsity Press.)

8. Consider how you can apply the Scripture to your life. Remember that the group will follow your lead in responding to the studies. They will not go any deeper than you do.

9. Once you have finished your own study of the passage, familiarize yourself with the leader's notes for the study you are leading. These are designed to help you in several ways. First, they tell you the purpose the study guide author had in mind when writing the study. Take time to think through how the study questions work together to accomplish that purpose. Second, the notes provide you with additional background information or suggestions on group dynamics for various questions. This information can be useful when people have difficulty understanding or answering a question. Third, the leader's notes can alert you to potential problems you may encounter during the study.

10. If you wish to remind yourself of anything mentioned in the leader's notes, make a note to yourself below that question in the study.

Leading the Study

1. Begin the study on time. Open with prayer, asking God to help the group to understand and apply the passage.

2. Be sure that everyone in your group has a study guide. Encourage the group to prepare beforehand for each discussion by reading the introduction to the guide and by working through the questions in the study.

3. At the beginning of your first time together, explain that these studies are meant to be discussions, not lectures. Encourage the members of the group to participate. However, do not put pressure on those who may be hesitant to speak during the first few sessions. You may want to suggest the following guidelines to your group.

☐ Stick to the topic being discussed.

☐ Your responses should be based on the verses that are the focus of the discussion and not on outside authorities such as commentaries or speakers.

☐ These studies focus on a particular passage of Scripture. Only rarely should you refer to other portions of the Bible. This allows for everyone to participate in in-depth study on equal ground.

☐ Anything said in the group is considered confidential and will not be discussed outside the group unless specific permission is given to do so.

☐ We will listen attentively to each other and provide time for each person present to talk.

☐ We will pray for each other.

4. Have a group member read the introduction at the beginning of the discussion.

5. Every session begins with a group discussion question. The question or activity is meant to be used before the passage is read. The question introduces the theme of the study and encourages group members to begin to open up. Encourage as many members as possible to participate, and be ready to get the discussion going with your own response.

This section is designed to reveal where our thoughts or feelings need to be transformed by Scripture. That is why it is especially important not to read the passage before the discussion question is asked. The passage will tend to color the honest reactions people would otherwise give because they are, of course, supposed to think the way the Bible does.

You may want to supplement the group discussion question with an icebreaker to help people get comfortable. See the community section of *Small Group Idea Book* for more ideas.

You also might want to use the personal reflection question with your group. Either allow a time of silence for people to respond individually or discuss it together.

6. Have a group member (or members if the passage is long) read aloud the passage to be studied. Then give people several minutes to read the passage again silently so that they can take it all in.

7. Question 1 will generally be an overview question designed to briefly survey the passage. Encourage the group to look at the whole passage, but try to avoid getting sidetracked by questions or issues that will be addressed later in the study.

8. As you ask the questions, keep in mind that they are designed to be used just as they are written. You may simply read them aloud. Or you may prefer to express them in your own words.

There may be times when it is appropriate to deviate from the study guide. For example, a question may have already been answered. If so, move on to the next question. Or someone may raise an important question not covered in the guide. Take time to discuss it, but try to keep the group from going off on tangents.

9. Avoid answering your own questions. If necessary, repeat or rephrase them until they are clearly understood. Or point out something you read in the leader's notes to clarify the context or meaning. An eager group quickly becomes passive and silent if they think the leader will do most of the talking.

10. Don't be afraid of silence. People may need time to think about the question before formulating their answers.

11. Don't be content with just one answer. Ask, "What do the rest of you think?" or "Anything else?" until several people have given answers to the question.

12. Acknowledge all contributions. Try to be affirming whenever possible. Never reject an answer. If it is clearly off-base, ask, "Which verse led you to that conclusion?" or again, "What do the rest of you think?"

13. Don't expect every answer to be addressed to you, even though this will probably happen at first. As group members become more at ease, they will begin to truly interact with each other. This is one sign of healthy discussion.

14. Don't be afraid of controversy. It can be very stimulating. If you don't resolve an issue completely, don't be frustrated. Move on and keep it in mind for later. A subsequent study may solve the problem.

15. Periodically summarize what the group has said about the passage. This helps to draw together the various ideas mentioned and gives continuity to the study. But don't preach.

16. At the end of the Bible discussion you may want to allow group members a time of quiet to work on an idea under "Now or Later." Then discuss what you experienced. Or you may want to encourage group members to work on these ideas between meetings. Give an opportunity during the session for people to talk about what they are learning.

17. Conclude your time together with conversational prayer, adapting the prayer suggestion at the end of the study to your group. Ask for God's help in following through on the commitments you've made.

18. End on time.

Many more suggestions and helps are found in *How to Lead a LifeGuide Bible Study.*

Components of Small Groups

A healthy small group should do more than study the Bible. There are four components to consider as you structure your time together.

Nurture. Small groups help us to grow in our knowledge and love of God. Bible study is the key to making this happen and is the foundation of your small group.

Community. Small groups are a great place to develop deep friendships with other Christians. Allow time for informal interaction before and after each study. Plan activities and games that will help you get to know each other. Spend time having fun together going on a picnic or cooking dinner together.

Worship and prayer. Your study will be enhanced by spending time praising God together in prayer or song. Pray for each other's needs and keep track of how God is answering prayer in your group. Ask God to help you to apply what you are learning in your study.

Outreach. Reaching out to others can be a practical way of applying what you are learning, and it will keep your group from becoming self-focused. Host a series of evangelistic discussions for your friends or neighbors. Clean up the yard of an elderly friend. Serve at a soup kitchen together, or spend a day working on a Habitat house.

Many more suggestions and helps in each of these areas are found in *Small Group Idea Book.* Information on building a small group can be found in *Small Group Leaders' Handbook* and *The Big Book on Small Groups* (both from InterVarsity Press). Reading through one of these books would be worth your time.

Before each study, you may want to put an asterisk by the key questions you think are most important for your group to cover, in case you don't have time to cover all the questions. As we suggested in "Getting the Most Out of *The Jesus Paul Knew*," if you want to make sure you have enough time to discuss all the questions, you have other options. For example, the group could decide to extend each meeting to ninety minutes or more. Alternatively, you could devote two sixty-minute sessions to each study.

Study 1. Source of Grace. 1 Timothy 1:1-2, 12-17.
Purpose: To establish the strong ties between Paul and Jesus and find in them a model for a personal relationship with Jesus.
Question 1. Paul has invested his life in his protégé, Timothy. In his two letters he wants Timothy not only to know Christian doctrine but to be convinced of the validity of Paul's credentials as a spokesman for Jesus. Paul qualified as an authoritative apostle of Jesus because he had obeyed God his Savior and Jesus his hope. Now he wants to be sure that Timothy is a true believer, and because he knew Timothy's faith was genuine he gave Timothy his blessing of grace, mercy, and peace. These are huge theological ideas, but this is not the appropriate setting to discuss them. Keep in mind the focus of these studies: Paul's knowledge of and walk with Jesus.
Question 4. Paul opened his heart to Timothy to show how deeply his life had been changed after he had come to know Jesus. His story begins with a pattern of praise and thanksgiving to Jesus. The details of his appointment will be discussed in study two, so you do not need to look them up now.
Question 5. Paul never tried to hide his sordid past, but rather recalled it to show he had experienced what it meant to be brought

into fellowship with Jesus. The classic meaning of *mercy* is that he did not receive the judgment he rightfully deserved, while *grace* means he did receive what he did not deserve. Scholars have tried to pin down exactly what Paul meant by his "ignorance and unbelief," and there are several opinions based on what Paul testified to at his trials. We will do an entire study on Philippians 3, which sheds light on what he meant by his ignorance. Keep moving toward the title of this study guide, *The Jesus Paul Knew*, and show how God's abundant grace poured out on Paul and the faith and love he found in Jesus connect with that idea.

Study 2. Visionary Leader. Acts 26.

Purpose: To discover the costs of Paul's relationship with Christ and how we must also be prepared to face similar costs in our walk with Jesus.

Question 1. Paul's story is also told by historian Luke in Acts 9:1-18 and by Paul himself in Acts 22:1-16. The main facts of each telling are the same although the settings vary.

Question 2. The decisive issue for Paul was the importance and value of how and why Jesus had changed his life. He wanted both secular and religious authorities to know. Paul could not possibly be what is sometimes called a secret believer.

Question 4. It is important to dig out all the facts because they shaped everything that was to come in Paul's relationship with Jesus. "I am Jesus" is the most important fact of all. Paul had no idea he was persecuting the Lord. Having met Jesus, he is ready for his assignment (vv. 16-18). Discuss how simple and clear Jesus made it to Paul (v. 16). He was to be his servant and witness. Put in your own words what Jesus was sending Paul to do, and show how this was a classic definition of the Christian gospel. "The power of Satan" shows beyond doubt that Jesus believed Satan was a real person who rules the powers of darkness.

Question 5. Summarize Paul's past from his own testimony (vv. 1-11). He cited his religious upbringing as a child and his strict life as a Pharisee as an adult. The Pharisees were the most devoted and strictest sect of the Jews, and they fell under severe criticism from Jesus. As a Pharisee, Paul led attacks against the early Christians. The resurrection of Jesus was now the cornerstone of Paul's faith, what he called his hope.

Question 8. This is not the place to criticize one another's churches. However, it is necessary to consider your church in light of Scripture.

Study 3. Comfort in Dark Times. Philippians 1:12-26.

Purpose: To discover how Jesus met Paul while he was in prison and what this says to us about our meeting Jesus in adversity.

Question 1. Paul wrote this letter to the church at Philippi to thank them for their gift of money. It is called a prison epistle because Paul had been imprisoned by Emperor Nero, but this letter sparkles with triumph and joy. "Spin" is not to be taken negatively, as it often is in our media. Rather, it describes how Paul made a hopeless situation into a hopeful one.

Question 2. Keep in mind the overall theme of this study: *The Jesus Paul Knew.* Look for the positives Paul found in Jesus. He made his personal acquaintance on the Damascus Road (Acts 26:12-19). This set his life's course and gave him purpose. His values led him to success as a witness and evangelist, teacher, writer, and driving force for new advances of the gospel for Jews and Gentles alike.

Question 3. Paul did not need new strategies to preach or to escape from prison. His bonds were his witness as the gospel spread. Jesus empowered him to be faithful to his calling by giving him courage, hope, and strength.

Question 5. "Rejoice" in this setting goes far beyond feeling good or happy. For Paul it was a deep-seated gratitude for what God was accomplishing through various witnesses in his prison. He knew Jesus was being proclaimed. That fact gave him intense satisfaction and joy from his sense of fulfilling his calling by Jesus.

Question 6. A quick review of the main points of study two would be helpful here. Make the connection clear between Paul's calling and his imprisonment.

Question 7. Paul's classic statement in verse 21 can easily become a cliché. Take time to explore the contemporary application of both parts of his resounding affirmation. "To live is Christ" (not *for* Christ) colored everything he did. He wanted to be known as a Jesus person. Seeing death as a "gain" filled him with peace as Jesus had promised (John 16:33).

Question 8. Paul had learned that being with Jesus was more important than his (Paul's) work. Apparently somehow Paul had picked up the truth of what Jesus had promised his disciples (John 14:1-3; 17:24).

Question 9. Here again we see how Paul's knowledge of Jesus kept him pushing his converts to the same high quality relationship. This simple triad—from Jesus to Paul to new Christians—was Paul's missional blueprint. To see his new converts abound in their boasting in their knowledge of Christ gave him his greatest reason for continuing to live. Explore how their boasting was a good thing for Paul and Jesus.

Study 4. The Peacemaker. 2 Corinthians 5:11-21.

Purpose: To discover Paul's peacemaking call from Jesus and what it means for Christians to be Christ's ambassadors.

Question 1. This passage is loaded with facts about a key component of the Paul-Jesus story. Make your list quickly without stopping to discuss each fact.

Question 2. Paul does not answer this question, so we have to use our imagination based on what we have learned about them so far. We gain fresh insights (call it imagination of your will) from re-creating the story. Pretend you are on the scene, taking and listening. Jesus promised us the Holy Spirit's guidance (John 14:25-27).

Question 3. "In Christ" describes Paul's relationship with Jesus throughout his letters. Basically, he pictures a strong friendship and partnership based on his deeply settled trust in Christ and his faithful obedience to his will. In verse 17 he takes a refreshing turn by claiming to be a new person in Christ. So powerful was their relationship that Paul said the old things of his past were gone, replaced by all new things. It was like giving up an old wreck of a car for a brand-new model right off the show room floor.

Question 5. Verses 18-19 introduce the concept of reconciliation: (1) Paul was reconciled to God by Jesus. (2) God gave Paul a ministry of reconciliation. (3) God is reconciling the world to himself and does not charge us with our sins. (4) God gave Paul the "message" of reconciliation that is the gospel. (5) Paul is now Christ's ambassador, begging people to be reconciled to God. Each fact merits serious discussion, but our task here is not to attempt to explain each truth fully but to show Paul's role with Jesus in God's program of bringing people to peace with himself.

Humankind's sin and God's righteousness constitute much of Paul's thinking (cf. Romans 1–5). He knew, of course, the connection between the cross of Jesus and our sin. In this letter he does not expound the entire doctrine, but he shows that our reconciliation with God is necessary because of our sin. The great trade off that sealed his salvation, which Paul had to learn, was Christ's becoming sin for him so that Paul might become God's righteousness.

Question 6. One way I learned to do this is to practice telling the Jesus story in simple English. I was taught to scrub the usual religious words and use words a non-Christian might better understand. Much of our biblical terminology is abstract and hard for the typical person to grasp.

Question 7. *Ambassador* was a role Jesus gave to Paul, but Paul only uses it twice in his correspondence (see Ephesians 6:20). Here it is most fitting because of the ministry Jesus gave to him in leading people to be reconciled to God.

Question 10. Paul's focus on Jesus was so sharp and personal that he saw himself taking the place of Jesus in urging people to be reconciled with God. To get the picture, read verse 21 like this: God made Jesus, who had no sin, to be sin for me, so that in him I might become the righteousness of God.

Study 5. Demanding Everything. Philippians 3:1-14.

Purpose: To learn from Jesus what it means to give him full control of every part of life.

Question 1. These verses show the immediate context of Paul's ministry at Philippi. Circumcision was the big issue because it stood for identification as a Jew who is loyal to the laws of Moses. This religious rite initiated with God's command to Abraham. Therefore it was a serious matter when some Christians decided to continue the practice, even though it violated the doctrine of salvation by faith and grace alone.

Question 2. *Flesh* here does not mean our physical body. It is used metaphorically to include our total human, sinful nature. This theological concept occurs frequently in Paul's letters. "For when we were in the realm of the flesh, the sinful passions aroused by the law were at work in us, so that we bore fruit for death" (Romans 7:5-6).

Question 3. Suggest some modern issues or religious traditions that would be similar to those at Philippi. Some of these may arise in an urban context, where debates rage over social and religious issues, such as "Is Jesus the only way?" Or issues of sexuality and social justice. Be careful not to spend too much time here because there is much to discover about Jesus.

Question 4. Paul moves from the problem at Philippi to his own conversion and finding the truth in Jesus. Again, he uses a powerful concept—*loss*. Your interviews should help to clarify Paul's move from his religious pedigree (vv. 4-6) to the supreme value of knowing Jesus as his Lord (vv. 7-8). This is where his learning about Jesus and his demands found its roots.

Question 5. *Value* has many meanings in secular culture. Television ads, for example, push the value of cars, floor cleaners, or whatever. Look for what is the most beneficial for how you live under Christ's demands.

Question 7. These verses are the heart of this study. Discover the facts about Jesus and Paul. Show how they are the groundwork for Paul's learning Christ's demands. Paul gloried in Jesus, even though he had many reasons to have "confidence in the flesh," especially because of his Jewish pedigree and observance. Jesus was far more important to him than all of his other assets put together. "For the sake of Christ" became the guiding star of his life. He aspired to follow Jesus in both his death and resurrection. The Jesus-Paul relationship is perhaps best pictured in Paul's desire to have Jesus "take hold" of him. Jesus was his goal in heaven. That's the kind of emotional attachment counselors love to see.

Question 8. Be clear about the two kinds of righteousness: (1) that which Paul and the religious Jews tried to attain by keeping the Old Testament laws, and (2) that which Paul attained by confessing faith in Jesus (Romans 3:21-26). Learn all you can about Jesus and the necessity of personal faith in him. Books about Jesus abound, but some of the clearest are *More Than a Carpenter* by Josh McDowell and *The Case for Christ* by Lee Strobel.

Question 9. Summarize these verses and emphasize the dramatic changes Paul's knowledge of Jesus brought into his life. Choose the fact that most clearly speaks to you about Jesus demanding everything of you.

Question 10. Paul's knowledge of Jesus reached the summit of his experience: (1) knowing the power of Christ's resurrection, and (2) sharing his sufferings. It is hard to put flesh and blood on what Paul learned. But his goals laid the foundation of meeting Christ's demands.

Study 6. Lover and Protector. Romans 8:31-39.
Purpose: To discover and live under Christ's love and protection for his glory and your good.

Question 1. Romans 8 takes us deep into Paul's knowledge of Jesus. Paul's relationship with Jesus is so profound that it has served as the Christian's source of peace and comfort in all circumstances. This chapter is a turning point in Paul's letter from doctrine (Romans 1–7) to his personal faith and knowledge of Jesus as his lover and protector. To prove his point, Paul pointed to the cross, where God gave us his Son. Thus, we can count on him to "give us all things." Paul's knowledge of Jesus flourished in the soil of the cross, where he saw Christ's love so magnificently.

Question 2. Jesus on the cross is Paul's key truth when it comes to our forgiveness and justification, which is God's gift of righteousness. Christ's love exonerated Paul and forgave all charges against him. He was set free from the condemnation he deserved. Christ's love for him pointed him toward heaven, where the risen Jesus intercedes for him. That is the love he learned.

Question 3. Paul's walk with Jesus took him from heaven to earth. There he found severe tests of his faith and more to learn about the love and protection of Jesus. Separation from Jesus and his love was possibly the worst thing he could imagine. In the text, "who" suggests people who would cause him troubles and hardship and cut him off from Jesus. But he did not exclude things he had no control over: famine, nakedness, danger, sword. They suggested Christ's love was at risk from these things, but Paul learned that Christ's love would endure.

Question 5. Paul was prepared for even the worst with Jesus (v. 36). He chose a vivid Old Testament metaphor to complete his picture. He faced death like an innocent sheep on the way to the slaughter house. He chose this saying from Psalm 44:22. Speaking of Jesus, Paul said he faced death every day. Nevertheless, Jesus was still his lover and protector.

Question 6. In a dramatic way, Paul chose to call himself more than a conqueror. Look at his list of experiences again. How could Paul be so sure Christ's love would make him *more* than a conqueror? Only by the strength, courage, and faith that Jesus had given to him. He was a conqueror "through him who loved us."

Question 9. Again Paul raised the possibility of his being separated from God's love in Christ. That would not happen because Jesus was his protector (vv. 38-39). Nothing in Scripture surpasses this assurance of Christ's protection. Nothing escapes his care. Jesus frees us from demonic powers and "anything else in all creation." Nowhere else do we find such an all-encompassing demonstration of Christ's love and power. This is what Paul learned at the feet of Jesus.

Study 7. Choosing the Cross. 1 Corinthians 1:18-31; 2:1-5.
Purpose: Allowing the cross of Jesus to shape one's faith, worship and habits.

Question 1. Read Acts 18:1-18 for Paul's story at Corinth. Corinth was a wealthy cosmopolitan commercial center. Many people there became believers, and Paul taught them for a year and a half. Corinthians generally followed pagan Greek philosophy, which Paul called "the wisdom of this age," which is "coming to nothing" (1 Corinthians 2:6). Of the new Christians at Corinth, he said, "not many of you were wise by human standards; not many were influential; not many were of noble birth" (v. 26). Obviously, Paul had learned much about the Corinthians, but they were "in Christ," and he learned that Jesus was their wisdom, righteousness, and redemption (v. 30).

Question 2. This question focuses on facts—the doctrinal truths about Jesus that Paul had to learn. The heart of our faith rests here. Do not try to explain the full meaning of each truth. Talk about the application of each one to your life.

Question 3. The relationship between Jesus and Paul rested on Paul's willingness to accept identification with Jesus, who seemingly lacked power. His commitment followed careful study of the records about Jesus, which he had to learn for his classes of new converts at Corinth. For Paul to learn from Jesus was much more than ideas about some new religion. It was extremely personal and could be quite embarrassing publicly.

Question 4. This question will force you to face the same issue Paul did with Jesus. How could the crucified Jesus possibly be the answer to the world's wisdom and my personal spiritual needs? The competition today among ideas about the meaning of the cross is fierce. Faith requires taking the same steps Paul did in deciding to follow Jesus, cross and all.

Question 5. The crux of the matter between Jesus and Paul lies here. Paul had to accept the paradox of Jesus dying on the cross and at the same time being God's power and wisdom. In one sense, these truths cannot be reconciled. Power and wisdom cannot possibly come from the cross, but that is the fundamental fact Paul learned from Jesus. There is indeed power and wisdom in the cross, impossible as that seems to us. But this truth became the heart of Paul's walk with Jesus. An old hymn makes it clear: "I must needs go home by the way of the cross. There's no other way but this; I shall ne'er get sight of the Gates of Light, if the way of the cross I miss" (Jessie Pounds, "The Way of the Cross Leads Home," 1906.)

Question 6. Jesus' teaching, which Paul embraced, included the radical idea that Jesus was fit for anyone. Paul had made his mark as a lecturer in the Athens Forum, among other places. It was expected that such traveling speakers and philosophers would draw responses from the upper classes, not from the nobodies. Paul learned from Jesus that people built personal relationships around his message of the cross. That was the chief value Paul had to learn.

Question 7. Look up and give simple definitions of big doctrines like wisdom, righteousness, holiness, and redemption. A good resource is IVP's *New Bible Dictionary* (Third Edition).

Paul related these truths to Jesus and the cross. They made a huge difference in his life and increased his knowledge of Christ and the cross. Keep your focus on the benefits Jesus gave Paul. These lessons were crucial to Paul's future preaching of the cross.

The *how* question requires our imagination because we do not have details about how their relationship actually succeeded.

Question 8. Paul introduces a practical tidbit (Jeremiah 9:24) to buttress his commitment to Jesus as his Lord. He learned from Jesus the difference between human boasting and boasting in Jesus. Jesus had taught him that God had "nullif[ied] the things that are, so that no one may boast before him" (vv. 28-29).

Paul could have boasted in his eloquence or superior wisdom (v. 1). But he chose to follow Jesus instead. He wanted to know nothing except his crucified Savior. That is how he sorted out his commitments. Knowing Jesus came first before anything else.

Question 9. This question requires a thorough examination of Paul's text. Keep in mind our central focus: what Paul learned from Jesus, especially about his crucifixion. Knowing Jesus made all the difference in the world for Paul. We see that the love, wisdom, and power of Jesus are most evident in Paul's life. For Paul, choosing the cross was a lifelong learning and growing process. Jesus loomed bigger and bigger in his life, making changes in Paul day-by-day.

Study 8. Giver of Strength and Contentment. Philippians 4:10-20.

Purpose: To find in Jesus strength, joy, and peace, regardless of the circumstances.

Question 1. "You sent me aid more than once" (v. 16). Paul did not specify what the gifts were, but considering he was a prisoner he had many needs: food, blankets, a warm cloak, writing materials, books, and even some cash. Paul's retelling of their gifts is spare, so that we might learn that the main issue for him was his spiritual contentment, *not* having enough to eat and so on.

Question 3. "In any and every situation" (v. 12), whether in times of need or times of plenty. Notice the extremes of his circumstances: well fed or hungry, plenty or want. It is hard to think that he could enjoy some interludes of relief in prison life, perhaps because of the believers' sharing with him.

Question 4. Examine the context in which Paul came to understand how his relationship with Jesus helped him to learn the secret of being content. Jesus was with him in everything, times when he had enough to eat and times when he was hungry. This is a secret known only to those who love and serve Jesus. The power of Jesus in Paul's life was great enough to enable him to do "all this." Paul did not write exactly what *all this* meant, but we know it included what we call good and bad times. He suffered hardships for Jesus, but he also found relief—strength and courage—through the gifts and prayers of his friends. Jesus was the Mediator of their gifts and prayers. Paul longed for them "with the affection of Christ Jesus" (Philippians 1:8).

Question 6. It is important to note how Paul gave significant roles to both Jesus (v. 13) and the Philippian Christians (v. 14) in finding his way through need and plenty. He discovered spiritual strength that comes only from Jesus; encouragement and love came from his friends. He needed both. He did not list his "troubles," but he needed the strength of Jesus to overcome whatever they were.

Question 7. Some popular ideas on television say you can't find contentment without strength. Paul's secret was that he enjoyed both; he was happy in Jesus, and he found peace, courage, joy, and hope in him. Strength does not necessarily mean physical ability, although a well-known Olympic runner made verse 13 his life verse. Discuss how this notion differs from Paul's. Careful application of this truth is required.

Question 9. Paul shifted attention from his needs to those of the Philippians, pointing them to Jesus where he had first learned Christ's riches. We can imagine what some of their needs were, but Paul seems to have their spiritual needs (v. 19) foremost in his thinking. What the Philippians gave to Paul was a fragrant sacrifice that pleased the Lord. "Riches . . . in Christ Jesus" is an abstraction. Go through the Gospel stories to find some of his riches. However we look at it, the fact is "God will meet all your needs." Paul had come to such a deep understanding of Jesus that he could refer to glorious wealth, right now, which gave him strength and contentment.

Study 9. Jesus or Nothing. Galatians 1:1-9; 2:20-21.

Purpose: To learn and apply what it cost Paul to be a complete learner of Jesus.

Question 1. The location of this letter is the Roman province of Galatia in Asia Minor. Paul preached the gospel there at least three times. Later on, some new converts challenged his leadership and teaching. This called Paul to write what he had learned from Jesus, the basic truth that salvation is by faith in Christ. At the same time, he traced his apostleship to his relationship with Jesus. His greeting reaffirms basic Christian truth: Jesus gave himself for our sins and to rescue us from the evil world. Therefore he is fully worthy of our praise (v. 5).

Question 2. Our relationship is based on the truth of the cross and the gifts of peace and grace from Jesus. It rests on hard historical evidence. Jesus really died for us, and we can know him personally like Paul did.

Question 4. Apostolic authority was a big issue for Paul. Notice that Paul's foundational truth about Jesus was his death and resurrection. This truth caused the Jews to suspect Paul's credentials. They were repelled by the idea of a crucified Savior. As Paul had learned about Jesus, they had to submit to his lordship. His was a divinely inspired mission carried out by the risen Savior who lived in Paul and the other believers.

Question 5. What Paul received from Jesus covers almost everything in his life and mission. He received much more than a bundle of historical facts; he received a living person. This was a life or death issue. "Gave himself for our sins" (v. 4) goes back to the Old Testament sacrifices to atone for sins, that is, to satisfy God's holiness and justice. "Rescue us" (v. 4) is a new idea, showing that Paul's life with Jesus threw a protective cover over him. Jesus had guaranteed such protection by his presence (Matthew 28:20; John 17:15).

Question 7. The idea that Christ died for nothing shot through the heart of Paul's life with Jesus. This false teaching simply obliterated not only the Jesus-Paul relationship but also the basic truth of salvation by faith and not by keeping the law. Paul taught this foundational truth in much greater detail in Romans 3:20-26. The false teaching was very attractive to the Jews because it allowed them to do works to obey God's rules and thus gain righteousness through the law. This approach to life simply nullified God's grace in Christ.

Question 9. This is perhaps our best picture of the Jesus-Paul relationship. It is intensely personal. You can well imagine Paul saying these things to his best friend, Jesus. You can get the feeling by saying, "I have been crucified with you. I no longer live because you live in me. I live by faith in you because you loved me and gave yourself for me." It is clearly Jesus or nothing. To appreciate and apply these facts is a life-changing experience; it is revolutionary and puts an end to law-keeping as the way of our salvation.

Study 10. Inspirer of Praise. Ephesians 1:3-14.
Purpose: To learn how to practice habits of praise privately and with your fellow Christians.

Question 1. Paul was no stranger to the practice of praise. His Old Testament worship was steeped in praise (see Psalm 145:3-7). Therefore, his new faith in Jesus easily led him to praise in response to God's greatness. Throughout Scripture praise is the believer's response to God's revelation of himself, which Paul had discovered afresh in Jesus. Believers recognize God's hand and acknowledge the one whose reality they have found. For Paul, that reality was Jesus. Paul thus joined believers throughout all time who have expressed their love for the Lord by praising him.

Question 2. Group leaders should have copies of the text ready for members at the time of study. This an excellent way to dig out the facts. It may seem elementary, but it works.

Question 3. Work to make abstract ideas clear. Such as "heavenly realms" and "every spiritual blessing." "Adoption to sonship" makes Paul's relationship with Jesus deeply personal. All of these facts draw Paul to clarify his purpose with Jesus: "to the praise of his glorious grace." Let the group meditate together on what this means.

Question 4. Encourage personal thoughts here. There are no right or wrong answers. Creativity is required when wrestling with Paul's ideas. There is no shame when it comes to admitting there are some things we cannot be totally sure about. This is a good time to ask God for his help. Keep in mind Paul's major phrase "in Christ Jesus" and its equivalent occur over thirty times in this letter.

Question 5. Apply some fresh, practical ideas about how praise works and what it looked like for Paul and Jesus. Paul included hymns (Colossians 3:16). Reading his letters was certainly part of a praise service. There was no musical accompaniment, but it wasn't long before readings of the psalms and the prophets became the foundation of Christian worship. Paul and Jesus were both saturated in the Psalms. We have no specific praise formats here, but Paul's benedictions are filled with praise (Romans 11:33-36; Ephesians 3:20-21).

Question 6. There are no right or wrong single meanings. What is important is our understanding of Paul's relation to Jesus. Note the basic fact that Paul's praise was inspired by "the One he loves," Jesus. Paul's relation with Jesus is wrapped up here in the words *redemption* and *forgiveness*.

Question 7. It's hard to link intimacy of relationship with doctrine. Paul and Jesus are a great example of how this can work for our good and God's glory.

Question 8. This is not the time for a full-blown discussion of the Holy Spirit's work. Suffice it to say that without the Spirit's work Paul would have not lived in vital connection with Jesus. The guaranteed deposit of the Spirit sealed their relationship. It gave ample reason to live to the praise of his glory.

Question 9. Note the words Paul used and connect them to reasons for his liberation: "every spiritual blessing," chosen "to be holy and blameless," "adoption to sonship," "grace," "redemption," "forgiveness," "riches of God's grace . . . lavished on us," "the promised Holy Spirit." Show how they fueled his life with Jesus.

James W. Reapsome (d. 2017) was a pastor for many years. He also served as editor of Evangelical Missions Quarterly *and the* World Pulse *newsletter. He was the coeditor of* Innovation in Mission *and the author or coauthor of LifeGuide studies such as* Exodus, Hebrews, Grief, Marriage, *and* Songs *from Scripture.*

What should we study next?

We have LifeGuides for . . .

LifeGuide® BIBLE STUDIES

KNOWING JESUS
Advent of the Savior
Following Jesus
I Am
Abiding in Christ
Jesus' Final Week
The Jesus Paul Knew
  (Spring 2018)

KNOWING GOD
Listening to God
Meeting God
God's Comfort
God's Love
The 23rd Psalm
Miracles
Questions God Asks
  (Fall 2018)

**GROWING IN
THE SPIRIT**
Meeting the Spirit
Fruit of the Spirit
Spiritual Gifts
Spiritual Warfare

**LOOKING AT
THE TRINITY**
Images of Christ
Images of God
Images of the Spirit

**DEVELOPING
DISCIPLINES**
Christian Disciplines
God's Word

Hospitality
The Lord's Prayer
Prayer
Praying the Psalms
Sabbath
Worship

**DEEPENING
YOUR DOCTRINE**
Angels
Apostles' Creed
Christian Beliefs
The Cross
End Times
Good & Evil
Heaven
The Kingdom of God
The Story of Scripture

SEEKERS
Encountering Jesus
Jesus the Reason
Meeting Jesus
Good News

LEADERS
Christian Leadership
Integrity
Elijah
Joseph

**SHAPING YOUR
CHARACTER**
Christian Character
Decisions
Self-Esteem

Parables
Pleasing God
Woman of God
*Women of the
  New Testament*
*Women of the
  Old Testament*

**LIVING FULLY
AT EVERY STAGE**
Singleness
Marriage
Parenting
*Couples of the
  Old Testament*
*Growing Older
  & Wiser*
Grandparenting

**REACHING
OUR WORLD**
Missions
Evangelism
Four Great Loves
Loving Justice

LIVING YOUR FAITH
Busyness
Christian Virtues
Forgiveness

**GROWING IN
RELATIONSHIPS**
Christian Community
Friendship

Find the perfect study for your group with IVP's LifeGuide Finder:
ivpress.com/lifeguidefinder